Owen Seaman

The battle of the bays

Owen Seaman

The battle of the bays

ISBN/EAN: 9783337731878

Printed in Europe, USA, Canada, Australia, Japan

Cover: Foto ©ninafisch / pixelio.de

More available books at **www.hansebooks.com**

THE BATTLE OF THE BAYS

BY OWEN SEAMAN

JOHN LANE
THE BODLEY HEAD
LONDON & NEW YORK   MDCCCXCVI

CONTENTS.

I. THE BATTLE OF THE BAYS:
                                                                             PAGE
    1. A Song of Renunciation 1
    2. For the Albums of Crowned Heads only . 5
    3. Marsyas in Hades 11
    4. The Rhyme of the Kipperling . . 15
    5. A Ballad of a Bun 22
    6. A Vigo-Street Eclogue 27
    7. An Ode to Spring in the Metropolis . 37
    8. Yet 42
    9. Elegi Musarum 44
II. TO MR. WILLIAM WATSON 49
III. ENGLAND'S ALFRED ABROAD 53
IV. LILITH LIBIFERA 57
V. ARS POSTERA 58
VI. A NEW BLUE BOOK 61
VII. TO A BOY-POET OF THE DECADENCE . . 64
VIII. TO JULIA IN SHOOTING TOGS 66

Contents.

		PAGE
IX.	The Links of Love	69
X.	Swords and Ploughshares	71
XI.	To the Lord of Potsdam	76
XII.	From the Lord of Potsdam	80
XIII.	'The Spacious Times'	83

I. THE BATTLE OF THE BAYS.

I.

A SONG OF RENUNCIATION.

(AFTER A. C. S.)

In the days of my season of salad,
    When the down was as dew on my cheek,
And for French I was bred on the ballad,
    For Greek on the writers of Greek,—
Then I sang of the rose that is ruddy,
    Of 'pleasure that winces and stings,'
Of white women and wine that is bloody,
    And similar things.

Of Delight that is dear as Desi-er,
    And Desire that is dear as Delight;
Of the fangs of the flame that is fi-er,
    Of the bruises of kisses that bite;

The Battle of the Bays.

Of embraces that clasp and that sever,
    Of blushes that flutter and flee
Round the limbs of Dolores, whoever
    Dolores may be.

I sang of false faith that is fleeting
    As froth of the swallowing seas,
Time's curse that is fatal as Keating
    Is fatal to amorous fleas;
Of the wanness of woe that is whelp of
    The lust that is blind as a bat—
By the help of my Muse and the help of
    The relative THAT.

Panatheist, bruiser and breaker
    Of kings and the creatures of kings,
I shouted on Freedom to shake her
    Feet loose of the fetter that clings;
Far rolling my ravenous red eye,
    And lifting a mutinous lid,
To all monarchs and matrons I said I
    Would shock them—and did.

The Battle of the Bays.

Thee I sang, and thy loves, O Thalassian,
    O 'noble and nude and antique!'
Unashamed in the 'fearless old fashion'
    Ere washing was done by the week;
When the 'roses and rapture' that girt you
    Were visions of delicate vice,
And the 'lilies and languors of virtue'
    Not nearly so nice.

O delights of the time of my teething,
    Félise, Fragoletta, Yolande!
Foam-yeast of a youth in its seething
    On blasted and blithering sand!
Snake-crowned on your tresses and belted
    With blossoms that coil and decay,
Ye are gone; ye are lost; ye are melted
    Like ices in May.

Hushed now is the bibulous bubble
    Of 'lithe and lascivious' throats;
Long stript and extinct is the stubble
    Of hoary and harvested oats;

The Battle of the Bays.

From the sweets that are sour as the sorrel's
   The bees have abortively swarmed ;
And Algernon's earlier morals
   Are fairly reformed.

I have written a loyal Armada,
   And posed in a Jubilee pose ;
I have babbled of babies and played a
   New tune on the turn of their toes ;
Washed white from the stain of Astarte,
   My books any virgin may buy ;
And I hear I am praised by a party
   Called Something Mackay !

When erased are the records, and rotten
   The meshes of memory's net ;
When the grace that forgives has forgotten
   The things that are good to forget ;
When the trill of my juvenile trumpet
   Is dead and its echoes are dead ;
Then the laurel shall lie on the crumpet
   And crown of my head !

2.

FOR THE ALBUMS OF CROWNED HEADS ONLY.

(AFTER SIR E. A.)

1. *From the third Sa'dine Box of the eighth Gazelle of Ghazal.*

YA YA! Best-Belovéd! I look to thy dimples and drink;
Tiddlihi! to thy cheek-pits and chin-pit, my Tulip, my Pink!

See my heart rises up like a bubble, and bursts in my throat,
And the dimples that draw it are Three, like the Men in a Boat.

Thrice Three are the Muses, and I that begat her should guess
That the Tenth is the TÉLE-EPHÉMERA, Pride of the PRESS!

The Battle of the Bays.

And the Graces were triplets till lately the fruitful
   Dîtî
Propagated a Fourth, and the infant was W.
   G.

From my post of Propinquity prone on my lan-
   guorous knees
My tears slither down like the Gum of Arabia's
   trees.

"Am I drunk?" Heart-Entangler! By Hafiz, the
   Blender of Squish!
'Tis the camel that sits on the prayer-mat is drunk
   as a fish.

As I hope for the future Uprising, deny it who
   can,
Two years I have worn the Blue Ribbon, come
   next Ramadan!

The Battle of the Bays.

Chest-Preserver! thou knowest thine eyes, they
    alone, are my drink,
Blue-black as the sloes of the Garden or Stephens
    his Ink.

On thy sugar-sweet liplets, my Cypress! I browse
    like a bee,
And am aching, as after a surfeit of Melon, for
    thee!

Low laid at thy feet—little feet—in the dust like a
    worm,
Round the train of thy skirt, O my Peacock, I
    fitfully squirm.

By Allah! I swoon, I rotate, I am sickly of hue!
And the Infidel swore that Jam-Jam was a Temper-
    ance brew!

Heart-Punisher! Surely I think it was jalapped
    with gin!
Aha! Paradise! I am passing! So be it! Amin!

2. *From a little thing by the Princess Onono Goawaï.*

>The bulbul hummeth like a book
>>Upon the pooh-pooh tree,
>And now and then he takes a look
>>At you and me,
>>At me and you.
>>>Kuchi !
>>>Kuchoo !

3. *From the Sanskrit of Matabíliwaijo.*

Wind ! a word with thee ! thou goest where my Well-Preservéd lies
On her bed of bonny briers keeping off the wicked flies.

Thou shalt know her by th' aroma of her bosom, which is musk,
And her ivories that glisten like an elephantine tusk.

The Battle of the Bays.

Seek her coral-guarded tympanum and whisper
 " Poppinjai ! "
And (referring to her lover) kindly add " A-lal-lal-
 lai ! "

Breeze ! thou knowest my condition ; state it
 broadly, if you please,
In a smattering of Indo-Turco-Perso-Japanese.

Say my youth is flitting freely, and before the sea-
 son goes
From the garden of my Tûtsi I am fain to pluck a
 rose.

Tell her I'm a wanton Sufi (what a Sufi really is
She may know, perhaps—I count it one of Allah's
 mysteries).

Fly, O blessed Breeze, and hither bring me back
 the net result ;
Fly as flies the rude mosquito from Abdullah's
 catapult.

The Battle of the Bays.

Fly as flies the rusty rickshaw of the Kurumaya-san,
When he scents a Hippopotam down the groves of Gulistan.

Fly and cull, O cull, a section of my Pipkin's purple tress;
Thou shalt find me drinking deeply with the Lords that rule the Mess;

Quaffing mead and mighty sodas with the Johnís, Lords of War,
Talking 'jungle in the gun-room,' underneath the deodar.

Hoo Tawâ! I go to join them; he that cometh late is curst,
For the Lords of War (by Akbar) have a most amazing thirst!

3.

MARSYAS IN HADES.

(AFTER SIR L. M.)

      NEXT I saw
A pensive gentleman of middle age,
That leaned against a Druid oak, his pipe
Pendent beneath his chin—a double one—
(Meaning the pipe); reluctant was his breath,
For he had mingled in the Morris dance
And rested blown ; but damsels in their teens,
All decorous and decorously clad,
Their very ankles hardly visible,
Recalled his motions ; while, for chaperon,
Good Mrs. Grundy up against the wall
Beamed approbation.

      On his face I read
Signs of high sadness such as poets wear,
Being divinely discontented with
The praise of *jeunes filles*. Even as I looked,
He touched the portion of his pipe reserved

The Battle of the Bays.

For minor poetry of solemn tone,
Checking the humorous stops intended for
Electioneering posters and the like;
And therewithal he made the following
Addition to his *Songs Unsung*, or else
His *Unremarked Remarks:*

      " Dear Sir," he said,
" Excuse my saying ' Sir ' like that; it is
Our way in Hades here among the damned;
For you must know that some of us are damned
Not only by faint praise but full applause
Of simple critics. Take my case. In me
Behold the good knight Marsyas, M.A.,
Three times a candidate for Parliament,
And twice retired; a Justice of the Peace;
Master of Arts (I said), and better known
In literary spheres as Master of
The Mediocre-Obvious; and read
By boarding-misses in their myriads.
These dote upon me. Sweetly have I sung
The commonplaces of philosophy
In common parlance.

The Battle of the Bays.

                You have read perhaps
The Cymric Triads? Poetry, they say,
Excels alone by sheer simplicity
Of language, subject, and invention. Sir!
The excellence of mine lay that way too.
But fate is partial. Heaven's fulgour moulds
' To happiness some, some to unhappiness ! '
(Look you, the harp was Welsh that figured forth
That excellent last line.) I ask you, Sir,
What would you? Ill content with mortal praise,
And haply somewhat overbold, I sought
To be as gods be; sought, in fact, to filch
Apollo's bays!

             Ah me! Dear me! I fain
Would use a stronger phrase, but hardly dare,
Being, whatever else, respectable.
I say I tired of vulgar homage, gift
Of ignorance. ' High failure overleaps
The bounds of low successes ' (there, again,
The harp that twanged was Welsh, but with an echo
Of Browning). Godlike it must be, I thought,

The Battle of the Bays.

To climb the giddy brink ; to pen, for instance,
An Ode to the Imperial Institute,
And fall, if bound to, from a decent height.

    I did and missed the laurel ; still I go
On writing ; what you hear just now is blank,
Distinctly blank, and might be measured by
The kilomètre ; yet I rhyme as well
A little ; but it takes a lot of time,
And checks the lapse of my pellucid stream
Not all conveniently."

                  Thereat he paused,
And wrung the moisture from his pipe ; but I,
As one that was intolerably bored,
Took even this occasion to be gone ;
And, going, marked him how he took his stile,
Polished the waxen tablets, and began
To make a Royal Pæan *by request*,
Or so he said.

4.

THE RHYME OF THE KIPPERLING.

(AFTER R. K.)

[N.B.—No nautical terms or statements guaranteed.]

AWAY by the haunts of the Yang-tse-boo,
    Where the Yuletide runs cold gin,
And the rollicking sign of the *Lord Knows Who*
    Sees mariners drink like sin;
Where the *Jolly Roger* tips his quart
    To the luck of the *Union Jack;*
And some are screwed on the foreign port,
    And some on the starboard tack;—
Ever they tell the tale anew
    Of the chase for the kipperling swag;
How the smack *Tommy This* and the smack *Tommy That*
They broached each other like a whiskey-vat,
    And the *Fuzzy-Wuz* took the bag.

The Battle of the Bays.

Now this is the law of the herring fleet that harries the northern main,
Tattooed in scars on the chests of the tars with a brand like the brand of Cain:
That none may woo the sea-born shrew save such as pay their way
With a kipperling netted at noon of night and cured ere the crack of day.

It was the woman Sal o' the Dune, and the men were three to one,
Bill the Skipper and Ned the Nipper and Sam that was Son of a Gun;
Bill was a Skipper and Ned was a Nipper and Sam was the Son of a Gun,
And the woman was Sal o' the Dune, as I said, and the men were three to one.

There was never a light in the sky that night of the soft midsummer gales,
But the great man-bloaters snorted low, and the young 'uns sang like whales;

The Battle of the Bays.

And out laughed Sal (like a dog-toothed wheel was
   the laugh that Sal laughed she):
"Now who's for a bride on the shady side of up'ards
   of forty-three?"

And Neddy he swore by butt and bend, and Billy
   by bend and bitt,
And nautical names that no man frames but your
   amateur nautical wit;
And Sam said, "Shiver my topping-lifts and scuttle
   my foc's'le yarn,
And may I be curst, if I'm not in first with a kip-
   perling slued astarn!"

Now the smack *Tommy This* and the smack *Tommy
   That* and the *Fuzzy-Wuz* smack, all three,
Their captains bold, they were Bill and Ned and
   Sam respectivelee.

And it's writ in the rules that the primary schools
   of kippers should get off cheap
For a two mile reach off Foulness beach when the
   July tide's at neap;

The Battle of the Bays.

And the lawless lubbers that lust for loot and filch
 the yearling stock
They get smart raps from the coastguard chaps with
 their blunderbuss fixed half-cock.

Now Bill the Skipper and Ned the Nipper could
 tell green cheese from blue,
And Bill knew a trick and Ned knew a trick, but
 Sam knew a trick worth two.

So Bill he sneaks a corporal's breeks and a belt of
 pipeclayed hide,
And splices them on to the jibsail-boom like a
 troopship on the tide.

And likewise Ned to his masthead he runs a rag of
 the Queen's,
With a rusty sword and a moke on board to bray
 like the Horse Marines.

But Sam sniffs gore and he keeps off-shore and he
 waits for things to stir,
Then he tracks for the deep with a long fog-horn
 rigged up like a bowchasér.

The Battle of the Bays.

Now scarce had Ned dropped line and lead when he spots the pipeclayed hide,
And the corporal's breeks on the jibsail-boom like a troopship on the tide ;
And Bill likewise, when he ups and spies the slip of a rag of the Queen's,
And the rusty sword, and he sniffs aboard the moke of the Horse Marines.

So they each luffed sail, and they each turned tail, and they whipped their wheels like mad,
When the one he said " By the Lord, it's Ned ! " and the other, " It's Bill, by Gad ! "

Then about and about, and nozzle to snout, they rammed through breach and brace,
And the splinters flew as they mostly do when a Government test takes place.

Then up stole Sam with his little ram and the nautical talk flowed free,
And in good bold type might have covered the two front sheets of the *P. M. G.*

But the fog-horn bluff was safe enough, where all was weed and weft,
And the conger-eels were a-making meals, and the pick of the tackle left
Was a binnacle-lid and a leak in the bilge and the chip of a cracked sheerstrake
And the corporal's belt and the moke's cool pelt and a portrait of Francis Drake.

So Sam he hauls the dead men's trawls and he booms for the harbour-bar,
And the splitten fry are salted dry by the blink of the morning star.

And Sal o' the Dune was wed next moon by the man that paid his way
With a kipperling netted at noon of night and cured ere the crack of day;
For such is the law of the herring fleet that bloats on the northern main,
Tattooed in scars on the chests of the tars with a brand like the brand of Cain.

The Battle of the Bays.

And still in the haunts of the Yang-tse-boo
Ever they tell the tale anew
  Of the chase for the kipperling swag ;
How the smack *Tommy This* and the smack
    Tommy That
They broached each other like a whiskey-vat,
  And the *Fuzzy-Wuz* took the bag.

The Battle of the Bays.

5.

A BALLAD OF A BUN.

(AFTER J. D.)

'I am sister to the mountains now,
   And sister to the sun and moon.'

'Heed not bellettrist jargon.'
JOHN DAVIDSON.

FROM Whitsuntide to Whitsuntide—
   That is to say, all through the year—
Her patient pen was occupied
   With songs and tales of pleasant cheer.

But still her talent went to waste
   Like flotsam on an open sea;
She never hit the public taste,
   Or knew the knack of Bellettrie.

Across the sounding City's fogs
   There hurtled round her weary head
The thunder of the rolling logs;
   "The Critics' Carnival!" she said.

The Battle of the Bays.

Immortal prigs took heaven by storm,
   Prigs scattered largesses of praise ;
The work of both was rather warm ;
   " This is," she said, " the thing that pays ! "

Sharp envy turned her wine to blood—
   I mean it turned her blood to wine ;
And this resolve came like a flood—
   " The cake of knowledge must be mine !

" I am in Eve's predicament—
   I sha'n't be happy till I've sinned ;
Away ! " She lightly rose, and sent
   Her scruples sailing down the wind.

She did not tear her open breast,
   Nor leave behind a track of gore,
But carried flannel next her chest,
   And wore the boots she always wore.

Across the sounding City's din
   She wandered, looking indiscreet,
And ultimately landed in
   The neighbourhood of Regent Street.

The Battle of the Bays.

She ran against a resolute
   Policeman standing like a wall ;
She kissed his feet and asked the route
   To where they held the Carnival.

Her strange behaviour caused remark ;
   They said, " Her reason has been lost ; "
Beside her eyes the gas was dark,
   But that was owing to the frost.

A Decadent was dribbling by ;
   " Lady," he said, " you seem undone ;
You need a panacea ; try
   This sample of the Bodley bun.

" It is fulfilled of precious spice,
   Whereof I give the recipe ;—
Take common dripping, stew in vice,
   And serve with vertu ; taste and see !

" And lo ! I brand you on the brow
   As kin to Nature's lowest germ ;
You are sister to the microbe now,
   And second-cousin to the worm."

The Battle of the Bays.

He gave her of his golden store,
   Such hunger hovered in her look;
She took the bun, and asked for more,
   And went away and wrote a book.

To put the matter shortly, she
   Became the topic of the town;
In all the lists of Bellettrie
   Her name was regularly down.

"We recognise," the critics wrote,
   "Maupassant's verve and Heine's wit;"
Some even made a verbal note
   Of Shakespeare being out of it.

The seasons went and came again;
   At length the languid Public cried:
"It is a sorry sort of Lane
   That hardly ever turns aside.

"We want a little change of air;
   On that," they said, "we must insist;
We cannot any longer bear
   The seedy sex-impressionist."

The Battle of the Bays.

Across the sounding City's din
   This rumour smote her on the ear :
" The publishers are going in
   For songs and tales of pleasant cheer ! "

" Alack ! " she said, " I lost the art,
   And left my womanhood foredone,
When first I trafficked in the mart
   All for a mess of Bodley bun.

" I cannot cut my kin at will,
   Or jilt the protoplastic germ ;
I am sister to the microbe still,
   And second-cousin to the worm ! "

6.

A VIGO-STREET ECLOGUE.

(AFTER THE SAME.)

Mæcenas. John. George. Arthur. Grant. Richard.

MÆCENAS.

What ho! a merry Christmas! Pff!
Sharp blows the frosty blizzard's whff!
Pile on more logs and let them roll,
And pass the humming wassail-bowl!

JOHN.

The wassail-bowl! the wind is snell!
Drinc hael! and warm the poet's pell!

MÆCENAS.

Richard! say something rustic.

RICHARD.
                          Lo!
The customary mistletoe,
Prehensile on the apple-bough,
Invites the usual kiss.

GEORGE.

                And now
Cathartic hellebore should be
A cure for imbecility.

GRANT.

Now holly-berries have begun
To blush for Women That Have Done.

ARTHUR.

The farmer sticks his stuffy goose!

MÆCENAS.

Come, come, you grow a little loose;
That's Michaelmas; you must remember
That Michaelmas is in September!

ARTHUR.

Northward the swallow sweeps his wing.

MÆCENAS.

No, no! the bird arrives in spring!

ARTHUR.

Such knowledge fits the country clown ;
We've better things to note in town.
What's Nature's lore compared with women's?

JOHN.

For this enigma go to S-m-ns ;
He is the——

ARTHUR.

      Yes, I am, I know,
The devil of a Romeo !

JOHN.

Hark ! hark ! the waits, the precious waits !
Their music beats at Heaven's gates.

MÆCENAS.

What Bodley wight will sing a stave
To match their strumming ? I would have
The manly bass of Hobbes's voice ;
But Unwin's house is Hobbes's choice.
George ! you've a baritone at need.

GEORGE.

Alas! my famous *Keynotes* lead
To *Discords*.

JOHN.

I've a little thing
Of *Resurrection*. Shall I sing?

ARTHUR.

Please do; but *à propos* of what?

JOHN.

I cannot say, unless *de bottes*.

[*Proceeds to sing a Ballad of Resurrection.*

A letter-card from my dear love!
   O folded page of blessed blue!
She burst her many-buttoned glove,
   And ripped the perforation through.

"My love, to-night, about eleven,
   With never a priest or passing-bell,
We die! and meet, with luck, in Heaven,
   But anyhow at least in Hell!"

The Battle of the Bays.

Her courage very nearly failed,
    In fact she swooned along the floor;
But curiosity prevailed,
    She came again and read some more.

" 'There is no way but this to choose;
    My people fain would have us wed;
But you and I have later views,
    And scorn the vulgar marriage-bed.

" Far be it from me to dictate
    How best to break the mortal bond,
But personally I may state
    That I shall use the village pond.

" Be punctual, love, and let us meet
    For weal or woe!
This line has lost a pair of feet;
    The post is now about to go."

Ay, ay, she thought, to meet were well,
    But if we found each other out?
You, say, in Heaven, I in Hell,
    Or else the other way about!

The Battle of the Bays.

Nay, there be heavy odds, she said,
    One fate shall save us both or damn;
We surely shall be bracketed!
    She ceased and sent a telegram.

To Guy le Preux de Balthazar—
    Here followed his address, and then
This pregnant message—"Right you are!"
    She wrote it with the office pen.

She flashed the phrase along the wires,
    Then, passing by a dagger-shop,
Bought one and wiped it on her sire's
    Best graduated razor-strop.

On second thoughts, she said, I lean
    To poison; true, a knife like this
Looks pretty, rib and rib between,
    But people very often miss.

She sought the chemist in his place;
    He sampled her with searching eye;
She looked him frankly in the face,
    And told a wicked, wicked lie.

The Battle of the Bays.

"My hen," she said,—"a bantam blend—
   Has hatched a poor demented chick;
To case the gentle creature's end
   I want a pint of arsenic."

The chemist deemed the order large,
   But said no thing and drew the drug;
She seized and bore the sacred charge
   Before her in a pewter mug.

At tea she faced her fell intent;
   Dressing, she lightly laughed at doom;
Dined with the family, and spent
   The evening in the drawing-room.

At ten the early rooster crowed;
   Ten-thirty struck and she was gone;
She crossed alone the naked road;
   The road had really nothing on.

Her golden braids hung down her back;
   Within her side she felt a stitch;
And once the moon behind the wrack
   Came out and caught her in a ditch.

The Battle of the Bays.

Once ere she reached the trysting-pear
    She broke the slumber of the rooks ;
She wrung her hands, she tore her hair,
    And did as people do in books.

From out her cloak she fetched the drug—
    "Thy health, my love, in Heaven or Hell!"
Deep to the dregs she drained the mug
    And dropped it, feeling far from well.

Upon the punctual stroke her fond
    True lover kept the oath he swore ;
Plunged softly in the village pond,
    But feeling chilly swam ashore.

Next morning in the judgment-place
    Two pallid prisoners were tried ;
Their guilt was plain ; it was a case
    Of ineffective suicide.

Yestreen a member of the Force
    Had found a woman deadly sick,
Lamenting, with sincere remorse,
    An overdose of arsenic.

Another heard upon his beat
  One darkly muttering, " This is Hell ! "
His weed was wet from head to feet ;
  He put him in a common cell.

The Justice chewed the evidence ;
  His eyes were soft, his lips were bland ;
It was, he said, a first offence ;
  He merely gave a reprimand.

" Go free, my poppets, keep the laws,
  And get ye wed at once," said he ;
The court indulged in rude applause ;
  The usher cleared the gallery.

The prison-warder, deeply stirred,
  Approached the culprits at the bar ;
Then haled them forth without a word
  Towards the nearest Registrar.

RICHARD.

John, you surpass yourself. Next week
Expect a flattering critique !

JOHN.

The waits are whining in the cold
With clavicorn and clarigold;
They play them like a crumpled horn,
The clarigold and clavicorn.

7.

AN ODE TO SPRING IN THE METROPOLIS.

(AFTER R. LE G.)

Is this the Seine?
And am I altogether wrong
About the brain,
Dreaming I hear the British tongue?
Dear Heaven! what a rhyme!
And yet 'tis all as good
As some that I have fashioned in my time,
Like *bud* and *wood;*
And on the other hand you couldn't have a more
    precise or neater
Metre.

Is this, I ask, the Seine?
And yonder sylvan lane,
Is it the *Bois?*
Ma foi!
Comme elle est chic, my Paris, my grisette!
Yet may I not forget

The Battle of the Bays.

That London still remains the missus
Of this Narcissus.

No, no! 'tis not the Seine!
It is the artificial mere
That permeates St. James's Park.
The air is bosom-shaped and clear;
And, Himmel! do I hear the lark,
The good old Shelley-Wordsworth lark?
Even now, I prithee,
Hark
Him hammer
On Heaven's harmonious stithy,
Dew-drunken—like my grammar!

And O the trees!
Beneath their shade the hairless coot
Waddles at ease,
Hushing the magic of his gurgling beak;
Or haply in Tree-worship leans his cheek
Against their blind
And hoary rind,

The Battle of the Bays.

Observing how the sap
Comes humming upwards from the tap-
Root !
Thrice happy, hairless coot !

And O the sun !
See, see, he shakes
His big red hands at me in wanton fun !
A glorious image that ! it might be Blake's,
Or even Crackanthorpe's !
For though the latter writes in prose
He actually is a bard ;
Yet Heaven knows
I find it passing hard
To think of any rhyme but *corpse*
For 'Crackanthorpe's.'

And O the stars ! I cannot say
I see a star just now,
Not at this time of day ;
But anyhow
The stars are all my brothers ;
(This verse is shorter than the others).

The Battle of the Bays.

O Constitution Hill !
(This verse is shorter still).

Ah ! London, London in the Spring !
You are, you know you are,
So full of curious sights,
Especially by nights.
From gilded bar to gilded bar
Youth goes his giddy whirl,
His heart fulfilled of Music-Hall,
His arm fulfilled of girl !
I frankly call
That last effect a perfect pearl !

I know it's
Not given to many poets
To frame so fair a thing
As this of mine, of Spring.
Indeed, the world grows Lilliput
All but
A precious few, the heirs of utter godlihead,
Who wear the yellow flower of blameless bodlihead !

The Battle of the Bays.

And they, with Laureates dead, look down
On smaller fry unworthy of the crown,
Mere mushroom men, puff-balls that advertise
And bravely think to brush the skies.
Great is advertisement with little men !
Moi, qui vous parle, L— G—ll—nn—,
Have told them so ;
I ought to know !

8.

YET.

(AFTER F. E. W.)

Sing me a drawing-room song, darling!
  Sing by the sunset's glow;
Now while the shadows are long, darling;
  Now while the lights are low;
Something so chaste and so coy, darling!
  Something that melts the chest;
Milder than even Molloy, darling!
  Better than Bingham's best.

Sing me a drawing-room song, darling!
  Sing as you sang of yore,
Lisping of love that is strong, darling!
  Strong as a big barn-door;
Let the true knight be bold, darling!
  Let him arrive too late;
Stick in a bower of gold, darling!
  Stick in a golden gate.

The Battle of the Bays.

Sing me a drawing-room song, darling!
    Bear on the angels' wings
Children that know no wrong, darling!
    Little cherubic things!
Sing of their sunny hair, darling!
    Get them to die in June;
Wake, if you can, on the stair, darling!
    Echoes of tiny shoon.

Sing me a drawing-room song, darling!
    Sentiment may be false,
Yet it will worry along, darling!
    Set to a tum-tum valse;
See that the verses are few, darling!
    Keep to the rule of three;
That will be better for you, darling!
    Certainly better for me.

9.

ELEGI MUSARUM.

(AFTER W. W.)

[To Mr. St. Loe Strachey.]

Dawn of the year that emerges, a fine and ebullient Phœnix,
  Forth from the cinders of Self, out of the ash of the Past;
Year that discovers my Muse in the thick of purpureal sonnets,
  Slating diplomacy's sloth, blushing for 'Abdul the d——d';
Year that in guise of a herald declaring the close of the tourney
  Clears the redoubtable lists hot with the Battle of Bays;
Binds on the brows of the Tory, the highly respectable Austin,
  Laurels that Phœbus of old wore on the top of his tuft;

The Battle of the Bays.

Leaving the locks of the hydra, of Bodley the numerous-headed,
  Clean as the chin of a boy, bare as a babe in a bath ;
Year that—I see in the vista the principal verb of the sentence
  Loom as a deeply-desired bride that is late at the post—
Year that has painfully tickled the lachrimal nerves of the Muses,
  Giving Another the gift due to Respectfully Theirs ;—
Hinc illæ lacrimæ ! Ah, reader ! I grossly misled you ;
  See, it was false ; there is no principal verb after all !

His likewise is the anguish, who followed with soft serenading
  Me as the tremulous tide tracks the meandering moon ;
Climbing as Romeo clomb, peradventure by help of a flower-pot,

The Battle of the Bays.

Where in her balconied bower lay, inexpressibly coy,
Juliet, not as the others, supinely, insanely erotic,
Pallid and yellow of hue, very degenerate souls,
Rioting round with the rapture of palpitant ichorous ardour,
But an immaculate maid, 'one,' you may say, 'of the best'!
His, I repeat, is the anguish—my journalist, eulogist critic,
Strachey, the generous judge, Saintly unlimited Loe!

Vainly the stolid *Spectator*, bewildered with fabulous bow-wows,
Sick with a surfeit of dog, ran me for all it was worth!
Vainly—if I may recur to a metaphor drawn from the ocean,
Long (in a figure of speech) tied to the tail of the moon—
Vainly, O excellent organ! with ample and aqueous unction

Once, as a rule, in a week, 'cleansing the Earth
 of her stain';
(Here you will possibly pardon the natural scion of
 poets,
 Proud with humility's pride, spoiling a passage
 from Keats)—
Vainly your voice on the ears of impregnable
 Laureate-makers,
 Rang as the sinuous sea rings on a petrified coast ;
Vainly your voice with a subtle and slightly indeli-
 cate largess,
 Broke on an obdurate world hymning the advent
 of Me ;
When from the 'commune of air,' from 'the ex-
 quisite fabric of Silence,'
 I, a superior orb, burst into exquisite print !

What shall we say for your greeting, O good horti-
 cultural Alfred !
 Royalty's darling and pride, crown of the Salis-
 bury Press ?
Now when the negligent Public, in search of a
 subject for dinner,

The Battle of the Bays.

Asks for the names of your books, Lord! what a boom there will be!
Hoarse in Penbryn are the howlings that rise for the hope of the Cymri;
Over her Algernon's head Putney composes a dirge;
Edwin anathematises politely in various lingos;
Davidson ruminates hard over a *Ballad of Hell;*
Fondly Le Gallienne fancies how pretty the Delphian laurels
Would have appeared on his own hairy and passionate poll;
I, imperturbably careless, untainted of jealousy's jaundice,
Simply regret the profane contumely done to the Muse;
Done to the Muse in the person of Me, her patron, that never
Licked Ministerial lips, dusted the boots of the Court!
Surely I hear through the noisy and nauseous clamour of Carlton
Sobs of the sensitive Nine heave upon Helicon's hump!

II. TO MR. WILLIAM WATSON.

[On writing the first instalment of *The Purple East*, a 'fine sonnet which it is our privilege to publish.' — *Westminster Gazette*, Dec. 16, 1895.]

DEAR Mr. Watson, we have heard with wonder,
   Not all unmingled with a sad regret,
That little penny blast of purple thunder,
   You issued in the *Westminster Gazette;*
The Editor describes it as a sonnet;
I wish to make a few remarks upon it.

Never, O craven England, nevermore
   Prate thou of generous effort, righteous aim!
So ran the lines, and left me very sore,
   For you may guess my heart was hot with shame:
Even thus early in your ample song
I felt that something must be really wrong.

The Battle of the Bays.

But when I learned that our ignoble nation
   Lay sleeping like a log, and lay alone,
Propping, according to your information,
   Abdul the Damned on his infernal throne,
O then I scattered to the wind my fears,
And nearly went and joined the Volunteers.

But just in time the thought occurred to me
   That England commonly commits her course
To men as good at heart as even we
   And possibly much richer in resource;
That we had better mind our own affairs
And leave these gentlemen to manage theirs.

It further seemed a work uncommon light
   For one like you, a casual civilian,
To order half a hemisphere to fight
   And slaughter one another by the million,
While you yourself, a paper Galahad,
Spilt ink for blood upon a blotting-pad.

The Battle of the Bays.

The days are gone when sword and poet's pen
    One gallant gifted hand was wont to wield ;
When Taillefer in face of Harold's men
    Rode foremost on to Senlac's fatal field,
And tossed his sword in air, and sang a spell
Of Roland's battle-song, and, singing, fell.

The days are gone when troubadours by dozens
    Polished their steel and joined the stout crusade,
Strumming, in memory of pretty cousins,
    The Girl I left behind Me, on parade ;
They often used to rattle off a ballad in
The intervals of punishing the Saladin.

In later times, of course I know there's Byron,
    Who by his own report could play the man ;
I seem to see him with his Lesbian lyre on,
    And brandishing a useful yataghan ;
Though never going altogether strong, he
Managed at least to die at Missolonghi.

The Battle of the Bays.

No more the trades of lute and lance are linked,
    Though doubtless under many martial bonnets
Brave heads there be that harbour the distinct
    Belief that they can manufacture sonnets;
But on the other hand a bard is not
Supposed to run the risk of being shot.

Then since your courage lacks a crucial test,
    And politics were never your profession,
Dear Mr. Watson, won't you find it best
    To temper valour with a due discretion?
That so, despite the fond *Spectator's* booming,
Above your brow the bays may yet be blooming.

III. ENGLAND'S ALFRED ABROAD.

[M. Alfred Austin, poète-lauréat d'Angleterre, vient d'arriver à Nice, où il a devancé la Reine. Il était, hier, dans les jardins de Monte-Carlo. Sera-ce sous notre ciel qu'il écrira son premier poème ?—*Menton-Mondain.*]

WRONG ? are they wrong ? Of course they are,
   I venture to reply ;
For I bore ' my first ' (and, I hope, my worst)
   A month or so gone by ;
And I can't repeat it under this
   Or any other sky.

What ! has the public never heard
   In these benighted climes
That nascent note of my Laureate throat,
   That fluty fitte of rhymes
Which occupied about a half
   A column of the *Times ?*

The Battle of the Bays.

They little know what they have lost,
  Nor what a carnal beano
They might have spent in the thick of Lent
  If only Daniel Leno
Had sung them *Jameson's Ride* and knocked
  The Monaco Casino.

Some day the croupiers' furtive eyes
  Will all be wringing wet;
Even the Prince will hardly mince
  The language of regret
At entertaining unawares
  The famed Alhambra Pet.

But still not quite incognito
  I mark the moving scene,
In a tepid zone where (like my own)
  The palms are ever green,
And find myself reported as
  A herald of the Queen.

The Battle of the Bays.

Here where aloft the heavens are blue,
    And blue the seas below,
I roll my eye and fondly try
    To get the rhymes to go,
As I pace *The Garden that I love*,
    Composing all I know.

But when my poet-pinions droop,
    And all the air is wan,
I enter in to the courts of sin
    And put a louis on,
And hold my heart and look again,
    And lo! the thing is gone!

Wrong? is it wrong? To baser crafts
    Has England's Alfred pandered,
Who once to the sign of Phœbus' shrine
    With awesome gait meandered,
And ever wrote in the cause of right
    According to his *Standard?*

The Battle of the Bays.

Nay ! this is life ! to take a turn
  On Fortune's captious crust ;
To pluck the day in a human way
  Like men of common dust ;
But O ! if England's only bard
  Should absolutely bust !

A laureate never borrows on
  His coming quarter's pay ;
And I mean to stop or ever I pop
  My crown of peerless bay ;
So I'll take the next *rapide* to Nice,
  And the 'bus to Cimiez.

MENTONE, *Feb.*, 1896.

IV. LILITH LIBIFERA.

EXHUMED from out the inner cirque of Hell
   By kind permission of the Evil One,
   Behold her devilish presentment, done
By Master Aubrey's weird unearthly spell!
This is that Lady known as Jezebel,
   Or Lilith, Eden's woman-scorpion,
   Libifera, that is, that takes the bun,
Borgia, Vivien, Cussed Damosel.

Hers are the bulging lips that fairly break
   The pumpkin's heart; and hers the eyes that
      shame
      The wanton ape that culls the cocoa-nuts.
Even such the yellow-bellied toads that slake
   Nocturnally their amorous-ardent flame
      In the wan waste of weary water-butts.

V. ARS POSTERA.

[On an advertisement of A Comedy of Sighs.*]*

Mr. Aubrey Beer de Beers,
   You're getting quite a high renown;
Your Comedy of Leers, you know,
   Is posted all about the town;
This sort of stuff I cannot puff,
   As Boston says, it makes me 'tired';
Your Japanee-Rossetti girl
   Is not a thing to be desired.

Mr. Aubrey Beer de Beers,
   New English Art (excuse the chaff)
Is like the Newest Humour style,
   It's not a thing at which to laugh;
But all the same, you need not maim
   A beauty reared on Nature's rules;
A simple maid *au naturel*
   Is worth a dozen spotted ghouls.

The Battle of the Bays.

Mr. Aubrey Beer de Beers,
   You put strange phantoms on our walls,
If not so daring as *To-day's*,
   Nor quite so Hardy as *St. Paul's;*
Her sidelong eyes, her giddy guise,—
   Grande Dame Sans Merci she may be;
But there is that about her throat
   Which I myself don't care to see.

Mr. Aubrey Beer de Beers,
   The Philistines across the way,
They say her lips—well, never mind
   Precisely what it is they say;
But I have heard a drastic word
   That scarce is fit for dainty ears;
But then their taste is not the kind
   Of taste to flatter Beer de Beers.

Bless me, Aubrey Beer de Beers,
   On fair Elysian lawns apart
Burd Helen of the Trojan time
   Smiles at the latest mode of Art;

The Battle of the Bays.

Howe'er it be, it seems to me,
    It's not important to be New;
New Art would better Nature's best,
    But Nature knows a thing or two.

Aubrey, Aubrey Beer de Beers,
    Are there no models at your gate,
Live, shapely, possible and clean?
    Or won't they do to 'decorate'?
Then by all means bestrew your scenes
    With half the lotuses that blow,
Pothooks and fishing-lines and things,
    But let the human woman go!

VI. A NEW BLUE BOOK.

[It was hardly to be supposed that the young decadents who once rioted . . . in the *Yellow Book* would be content to remain in obscurity after the metamorphosis of that periodical and the consequent exclusion of themselves. The *Savoy*, we learn, to be edited by Mr. Arthur Symons and Mr. Aubrey Beardsley, will appear early in December.—*Globe*.]

' THE world's great age begins anew,'
   Cold virtue's weeds are cast ;
Our heads are light, our tales are blue,
   And things are moving fast ;
And no one any longer quarrels
With anybody else's morals.

A racier journal stamps its pages
   With Beardsleys braver far ;
A bolder Editor engages
   To shame the morning star,
On *London Nights*, not near so chilly,
Sampling a shadier Piccadilly.

The Battle of the Bays.

Satyr and Faun their late repose
   Now burst like anything ;
New Mænads, turning sprightlier toes,
   Enjoy a jauntier fling ;
With lustier lips old Pan shall play
Drain-pipes along the sewer's way.

Priapus, wrongly left for dead,
   Is dead no more than Pan ;
Silenus rises from his bed
   And hiccups like a man ;
There's something rather chaste (between us)
About Priapus and Silenus.

O cease to brew your Bodley pap
   Whence all the spice is spent !
The splendour of its primal tap
   Was gone when Aubrey went ;
Behold that subtle Sphinx prepare
Fresh liquors fit to lift your hair.

The Battle of the Bays.

Another Magazine shall rise
    And paint the palsied town,
Of humbler hue, of simpler size,
    And sold at half a crown;
Please note the pregnant brand—*Savoy*,
And don't confuse with *saveloy.**

---

* Saveloy, a kind of sausage; French *cervelas*, from its containing brains.—SKEAT.

VII. TO A BOY-POET OF THE DECADENCE.

[Showing curious reversal of epigram—' La nature l'a fait sanglier ; la civilisation l'a réduit à l'état de cochon.']

But my good little man, you have made a mistake
   If you really are pleased to suppose
That the Thames is alight with the lyrics you make ;
   We could all do the same if we chose.

From Solomon down, we may read, as we run,
   Of the ways of a man and a maid ;
There is nothing that's new to us under the sun,
   And certainly not in the shade.

The erotic affairs that you fiddle aloud
   Are as vulgar as coin of the mint ;
And you merely distinguish yourself from the crowd
   By the fact that you put 'em in print.

The Battle of the Bays.

You're a 'prentice, my boy, in the primitive stage,
    And you itch, like a boy, to confess :
When you know a bit more of the arts of the age
    You will probably talk a bit less.

For your dull little vices we don't care a fig,
    It is *this* that we deeply deplore ;
You were cast for a common or usual pig,
    But you play the invincible bore.

VIII. TO JULIA IN SHOOTING TOGS

and a Herrickose vein.

Whenas to shoot my Julia goes,
Then, then, (methinks) how bravely shows
That rare arrangement of her clothes!

So shod as when the Huntress Maid
With thumping buskin bruised the glade,
She moveth, making earth afraid.

Against the sting of random chaff
Her leathern gaiters circle half
The arduous crescent of her calf.

Unto th' occasion timely fit,
My love's attire doth show her wit,
And of her legs a little bit.

The Battle of the Bays.

Sorely it sticketh in my throat,
She having nowhere to bestow't,
To name the absent petticoat.

In lieu whereof a wanton pair
Of knickerbockers she doth wear,
Full windy and with space to spare.

Enlargéd by the bellying breeze,
Lord! how they playfully do ease
The urgent knocking of her knees!

Lengthways curtailéd to her taste
A tunic circumvents her waist,
And soothly it is passing chaste.

Upon her head she hath a gear
Even such as wights of ruddy cheer
Do use in stalking of the deer.

Haply her truant tresses mock
Some coronal of shapelier block,
To wit, the bounding billy-cock.

The Battle of the Bays.

Withal she hath a loaded gun,
Whereat the pheasants, as they run,
Do make a fair diversión.

For very awe, if so she shoots,
My hair upriseth from the roots,
And lo! I tremble in my boots!

IX. THE LINKS OF LOVE.

My heart is like a driver-club,
   That heaves the pellet hard and straight,
That carries every let and rub,
   The whole performance really great ;
My heart is like a bulger-head,
   That whiffles on the wily tee,
Because my love has kindly said
   She'll halve the round of life with me.

My heart is also like a cleek,
   Resembling most the mashie sort,
That spanks the object, so to speak,
   Across the sandy bar to port ;
And hers is like a putting-green,
   The haven where I boast to be,
For she assures me she is keen
   To halve the round of life with me.

Raise me a bunker, if you can,
    That beetles o'er a deadly ditch,
Where any but the bogey-man
    Is practically bound to pitch;
Plant me beneath a hedge of thorn,
    Or up a figurative tree,
What matter, when my love has sworn
    To halve the round of life with me?

X. SWORDS AND PLOUGHSHARES.

Part I. Presto Furioso.

Spontaneous Us!
O my Camarados! I have no delicatesse as a
    diplomat, but I go blind on Libertad!
Give me the flap-flap of the soaring Eagle's pin-
    ions!
Give me the tail of the British lion tied in a knot
    inextricable, not to be solved anyhow!
Give me a standing army (I say 'give me,' because
    just at present we want one badly, armies
    being often useful in time of war).

I see our superb fleet (I take it that we are to have
    a superb fleet built almost immediately);
I observe the crews prospectively; they are con-
    stituted of various nationalities, not necessa-
    rily American;
I see them sling the slug and chew the plug;
I hear the drum begin to hum;

The Battle of the Bays.

Both the above rhymes are purely accidental and contrary to my principles.
We shall wipe the floor of the mill-pond with the scalps of able-bodied British tars!
I see Professor Edison about to arrange for us a torpedo-hose on wheels, likewise an infernal electro-semaphore;
I see Henry Irving dead-sick and declining to play Corporal Brewster;
Cornell, I yell! I yell Cornell!

I note the Manhattan boss leaving his dry-goods store and investing in a small Gatling-gun and a ten-cent banner;
I further note the Identity evolved out of forty-four spacious and thoughtful States;
I note Canada as shortly to be merged in that Identity; similarly Van Diemen's Land, Gibraltar and Stratford-on-Avon;
Briefly, I see Creation whipped!

O ye Colonels! I am with you (I too am a Colonel and on the pension-list);

I drink to the lot of you; to Colonels Cleveland,
 Hitt, Vanderbilt, Chauncey M. Depew, O'Don-
 ovan Rossa and the late Colonel Monroe;
I drink an egg-flip, a morning-caress, an eye-
 opener, a maiden-bosom, a vermuth-cocktail,
 three sherry-cobblers and a gin-sling!
Good old Eagle!

PART II. INTERMEZZO DOLOROSO.

[Allowing time for the fall of American securities to the extent of some odd hundred millions sterling; also for the Day of Rest.]

PART III. ANDANTE AMABILE.

Who breathed a word of war?
Why, surely we are men and Plymouth brothers!
Pray, what in thunder should we cut each other's
 Carotids for?

Merciful powers forefend!
For we by gold-edged bonds are bound alway,
Besides a lot of things that never pay
 A dividend!

The Battle of the Bays.

    Christmas! we cry thee *Ave!*
At such a time, when hearts with love are filled,
It seems inopportune for us to build
        The needful navy.

    In fact in many a church
Uprise the prayer and supplicating psalm
That Heaven would keep our spreading Eagle calm
        Upon his perch.

    Goodwill and peace and plenty!
Our leading congregations here agree
To vote for this arrangement, *nemine*
        Contradicente.

    Greatly be they extolléd
Who occupied the tabernacle-chair
And put it to the meeting then and there
        And passed it solid!

    That print has also played
A useful part that sent an invitation
To Redmond to relieve the situation
        (Answer prepaid).

The Battle of the Bays.

    Say, Sirs, and shall we sever?
And mar the fair exchange of fatted steers,
Chicago pig, and eligible peers?
        No! never, never!

    , Shall gore be made to flow?
Like kindred Sohrabs shall we knock our Rustums,
And blast our beautiful McKinley customs?
        Lord love us! no!

    Then, burst the sundering bar!
Our punctured pockets yearn across the ocean;
Till now we never had the faintest notion
        How dear you are!

    O love of other years!
Wall Street, aweary for her broken bliss,
Waits like a loving crocodile to kiss
        Again with tears!

XI. TO THE LORD OF POTSDAM.

[On sending a certain telegram.]

MAJESTIC Monarch! whom the other gods,
   For fear of their immediate removal,
Consulting hourly, seek your awful nod's
      Approval;

Lift but your little finger up to strike,
   And lo! 'the massy earth is riven' (Shelley),
The habitable globe is shaken like
      A jelly.

By your express permission for the last
   Eight years the sun has regularly risen;
And editors, that questioned this, have passed
      To prison.

In Art you simply have to say, "I shall!"
   Beethoven's fame is rendered transitory;
And Titian cloys beside your clever all-
      -egory.

The Battle of the Bays.

We hailed you Admiral : your eagle sight
   Foresaw Her Majesty's benign intentions ;
A uniform was ready of the right
      Dimensions.

Your wardrobe shines with all the shapes and
      shades,
   That genius can fix in fancy suitings ;
For *levées*, false alarums, full parades
      And shootings.

But save the habit marks the man of gore
   Your spurs are yet to win, my callow Kaiser !
Of fighting in the field you know no more
      Than I, Sir !

When Grandpapa was thanking God with hymns
   For gallant Frenchmen dying in the ditches,
Your nurse had barely braced your little limbs
      In breeches.

The Battle of the Bays.

And doubtless, where he roosts beside his bock,
    The Game Old Bird that played the leading
        fiddle
Smiles grimly as he hears your perky cock-
    -a-diddle.

Be well advised, my youthful friend, abjure
    These tricks that smack of Cleon and the tan-
        ners ;
And let the Dutch instruct a German Boor
    In manners.

Nor were you meant to solve the nations' knots,
    Or be the Earth's Protector, willy-nilly ;
You only make yourself and royal Pots-
    -dam silly.

Our racing yachts are not at present dressed
    In bravery of bunting to amuse you,
Nor can the licence of an honoured guest
    Excuse you.

The Battle of the Bays.

But if your words are more than wanton play
    And you would like to meet the old sea-rover,
Name any course from Delagoa Bay
        To Dover.

Meanwhile observe a proper reticence ;
    We ask no more ; there never was a rumour
Of asking Hohenzollerns for a sense
        Of humour !

XII. FROM THE LORD OF POTSDAM.

WE, William, Kaiser, planted on Our throne
By heaven's grace, but chiefly by Our own,
Do deign to speak. Then let the earth be dumb,
And other nations cease their senseless hum !
   Seldom, if ever, does a chance arise
For Us to pose before Our people's eyes ;
But this is one of them, this natal day
Whereon Our Ancient and Imperial sway,
Which to the battle's death-defying trump
Welded the States in one confounded lump,
(As many tasty meats are blent within
The German sausage's encircling skin)
By Our decree is twenty-five precisely,
And, under Us (and God) still doing nicely.
   Therefore ye Princelings, Plenipotentates,
And Representatives of various States,
A cool Imperial pint your Kaiser drains,
Both to Our 'more immediate' domains,
And to Our lands, Our isles beyond the sea,
Our World-embracing Greater Germany !

The Battle of the Bays.

Let loose the breathings of Our Royal Band,
We give a rouse—*hoch ! hoch !*—to HELIGOLAND !
[*Kaiserliche Kapelle* plays : *O Heligoland! mein Heligoland!* Air—*Die Wacht am Rhein.*]
    WILLIAM, KAISER, continues :—
There are that languish on this festal day
Damned and impounded for *lèse-majesté;*
We, William, in Our plenitude of grace,
Propose to pardon every hundredth case ;
And though their sentence was no more than just
We offer each a copy of Our bust,
With option of a fine ; but, be it known,
Whoso again shall deem his life his own,
Or find in Ours the faintest flaw or fleck,
God helping, We will hang him by the neck.
Yea, he shall surely curse his impious star
That dares to question Who or where We are !
Worship your Cæsar, and (C.V.) your God ;
Who spares the child may haply spoil the rod.
    Many Our uniforms, but We are one,
And one Our empire over which the sun,
Careering on his cloud-compulsive way,
Sets once, but never more than once, a day.

The Battle of the Bays.

The seas are Ours : world-wide upon the oceans
Our fleet commands the liveliest emotions;
Go where you will, you find Our German manners
Prevailing under other people's banners;
Go where you will, you cannot but remark
The cheap, but never nasty, German clerk;
Observe Our exports; do you ever see
Things made as they are made in Germany?
Always at home on Earth's remotest shores
E.g., among Our loved, low-German Boers,
Freely Our folk expectorate, and there
Our German bands inflame the balmy air;
Likewise again Our passionate bassoons
Tickle the niggers of the Cameroons;
Or others over whom Our Eagle flaps
In places not at present on the maps.
 One more Imperial pint! your Kaiser drinks
To German intercourse with missing links!
Let loose the breathings of Our Royal Band,
We give—*hoch! hoch!*—Our glorious HINTERLAND!
 [*Kaiserliche Kapelle* plays : *O Hinterland! mein Hinterland!* (Air as before); during which WILLIAM, KAISER, resumes his throne.]

XIII. 'THE SPACIOUS TIMES.'

[On Drake's return from his filibustering expedition of 1580 the Queen went on board his ship at Deptford, and after partaking of a banquet conferred on him the honour of knighthood, at the same time declaring herself mightily pleased with all that he had done.]

I WISH that I had flourished then,
    When ruffs and raids were in the fashion,
When Shakespeare's art and Raleigh's pen
    Encouraged patriotic passion ;
For though I draw my happy breath
    Beneath a Queen as good and gracious,
The times of Great Elizabeth
    Were more conveniently spacious.

Large-hearted age of cakes and ale !
    When, undeterred by nice conditions,
Good Master Drake would lightly sail
    On little privateer commissions ;
Careering round with sword and flame
    And no pretence of polished manners,
He planted out in England's name
    A most refreshing lot of banners.

The Battle of the Bays.

Blest era, when the reckless tar,
    Elated by a sense of duty,
Feared not to face his country's Bar
    But freely helped himself to booty;
Returning home with bulging hold
    The Queen would meet him, much excited,
Pronounce him worth his weight in gold
    And promptly have the hero knighted.

No Extra Special, piping hot,
    Broke out in unexpected Pyrrhics;
No Poet Laureate on the spot
    Composed apologetic lyrics;
Transpiring slowly by-and-by,
    The act was voted one of loyalty;
The nation winked the other eye,
    And pocketed the usual royalty.

Ere Reuter yet had found his range,
    These trifles done across the ocean
Produced upon the Stock Exchange
    No preternatural emotion;

The Battle of the Bays.

Not yet the Kaiserlich I AM
   Made wingéd words and then repented;
He wrote as yet no telegram,
   Nor was, in fact, himself invented.

No Justice Hawkins gauged the fault
   Of irresponsible incursions;
The early Hawkins, gallant salt,
   Knew well the charm of such diversions;
Men never saw that moving sight
   When legal luminaries muster,
And very solemnly indict
   A well-conducted filibuster.

No Member had the hardy nerve
   To criticise our depredations
As unadapted to preserve
   The perfect comity of nations;
No High Commissioner would doubt
   If brigandage was quite judicial;
Indeed we mostly did without
   This rather eminent Official.

No Ministry would care a rap
   For theoretic arbitration ;
They simply modified the map
   To meet the latest annexation ;
And so without appeal to law,
   Or other needless waste of tissue,
The Lion, where he put his paw,
   Remained and propagated issue.

To-day we wax exceeding fat
   On lands our roving fathers raided ;
And blush with holy horror at
   Their lawless sons who do as they did ;
No doubt the age improves a lot,
   It grows more honest, more veracious ;
But, as I said, the times are not
   Quite so conveniently spacious.

NOTE

To the Editors of *The World* and *The National Observer*, and to the Proprietors of *Punch*, I wish to express my thanks for their courtesy in permitting me to republish these verses.   O. S.

BY THE SAME AUTHOR.

Horace at Cambridge

A. D. INNES, Bedford Street, London.   3s. 6d. *net.*

'To every university man . . . this book will be a rare treat. But in virtue of its humour, its extreme and felicitous dexterity of workmanship both in rhyme and metre . . . it will appeal to a far wider public.'
—*Punch.*

'We very cordially recommend Mr. Seaman's book . . . to all who are likely to care for verse which is not unworthy to be ranked with the efforts of Calverley the immortal.'—*The World.*

'Mr. Seaman manages his ingenious metres with unfailing skill.'
—*The Athenæum.*

'A genial cynic with a genuine smack of Bon Gaultier.'
—*St. James's Gazette.*

'The humour is bright and spontaneous.'—*The Times.*

'Mr. Seaman's book is never slipshod; it has the neatness, the precision, the sparkle of its Latin namesake.'—*The Spectator.*

Tillers of the Sand

SMITH, ELDER & Co., London.   3s. 6d.

'In the political sphere Mr. Seaman is at present without a rival.'
—*The Globe.*

'Taken as a whole, we are much mistaken if any better volume of political verse has made its appearance since the days of the *Rolliad* and the *Anti-Jacobin.*'—*The World.*

'The best of the satirists on the other side is Mr. Owen Seaman, who has touched off some of the weaknesses of the late government with very happy and caustic humour.'—*The Spectator.*

'Mr. Seaman is own brother to Calverley, and in modern times there has been nothing so good of its sort as "Tillers of the Sand." . . . Mr. Seaman proves himself so brilliant a jester that it needs must be he takes the jester's privilege of offending no one.'—*The Speaker.*

'One of the most accomplished of writers of occasional verse to-day.'
—*Bookman.*

'It is all so good that passages are hard to choose.'—*Scotsman.*

'The author's rare quality—a capacity for satirizing one's political opponents with a wit that leaves no wound.'
—Mr. JAMES PAYN in *The Illustrated London News.*

'Brilliant and inimitable.'—*Chicago Daily News.*

List of Books
IN
BELLES LETTRES
Published by John Lane
The Bodley Head
VIGO STREET, LONDON, W.

Adams (Francis).
ESSAYS IN MODERNITY. Crown 8vo. 5s. net. [*Shortly.*
A CHILD OF THE AGE. (*See* KEYNOTES SERIES.)

A. E.
HOMEWARD SONGS BY THE WAY. Sq. 16mo, wrappers. 1s. 6d. net. *Transferred to the present Publisher.* [*Second Edition.*

Aldrich (T. B.).
LATER LYRICS. Sm. Fcap. 8vo. 2s. 6d. net.

Allen (Grant).
THE LOWER SLOPES: A Volume of Verse. With Title-page and Cover Design by J. ILLINGWORTH KAY. Crown 8vo. 5s. net.
THE WOMAN WHO DID. (*See* KEYNOTES SERIES.)
THE BRITISH BARBARIANS. (*See* KEYNOTES SERIES.)

Arcady Library (The).
A Series of Open-Air Books. Edited by J. S. FLETCHER. With Cover Designs by PATTEN WILSON. Each volume crown 8vo. 5s. net.
  I. ROUND ABOUT A BRIGHTON COACH OFFICE. By MAUDE EGERTON KING. With over 30 Illustrations by LUCY KEMP-WELCH.
  II. LIFE IN ARCADIA. By J. S. FLETCHER. Illustrated by PATTEN WILSON.

Arcady Library (The)—*cont.*
  III. SCHOLAR GIPSIES. By JOHN BUCHAN. With 7 full-page Etchings by D. Y. CAMERON
The following is in preparation:
  IV. IN THE GARDEN OF PEACE. By HELEN MILMAN. With Illustrations by EDMUND H. NEW.

Beeching (Rev. H. C.).
IN A GARDEN; Poems. With Title-page designed by ROGER FRY. Crown 8vo. 5s. net.
ST. AUGUSTINE AT OSTIA. Crown 8vo, wrappers. 1s. net.

Beerbohm (Max).
THE WORKS OF MAX BEERBOHM. With a Bibliography by JOHN LANE. Sq. 16mo. 4s. 6d. net.

Benson (Arthur Christopher)
LYRICS. Fcap. 8vo, buckram. 5s. net.
LORD VYET AND OTHER POEMS. Fcap. 8vo. 3s. 6d. net.

Bodley Head Anthologies (The).
Edited by ROBERT H. CASE. With Title-page and Cover Designs by WALTER WEST. Each volume crown 8vo. 5s. net.
  I. ENGLISH EPITHALAMIES. By ROBERT H. CASE.

THE PUBLICATIONS OF

Bodley Head Anthologies (The)—*continued.*
  II. MUSA PISCATRIX. By JOHN BUCHAN. With 6 Etchings by E. PHILIP PIMLOTT.
  III. ENGLISH ELEGIES. By JOHN C BAILEY.
  IV. ENGLISH SATIRES. By CHAS. HILL DICK.

Bridges (Robert).
  SUPPRESSED CHAPTERS AND OTHER BOOKISHNESS. Crown 8vo. 3s. 6d. net. [*Second Edition.*

Brotherton (Mary).
  ROSEMARY FOR REMEMBRANCE. With Title-page and Cover Design by WALTER WEST. Fcap. 8vo. 3s. 6d. net.

Crackanthorpe (Hubert).
  VIGNETTES. A Miniature Journal of Whim and Sentiment. Fcap. 8vo, boards. 2s. 6d. net.

Crane (Walter).
  TOY BOOKS. Re-issue, each with new Cover Design and End Papers. This LITTLE PIG'S PICTURE BOOK, containing:
    I. THIS LITTLE PIG.
    II. THE FAIRY SHIP.
    III. KING LUCKIEBOY'S PARTY.
  The three bound in one volume with a decorative cloth cover, end papers, and a newly written and designed preface and title-page. 3s. 6d. net; separately 9d. net each.
    MOTHER HUBBARD'S PICTURE BOOK, containing:
    I. MOTHER HUBBARD'S.
    II. THE THREE BEARS.
    III. THE ABSURD A. B. C.
  The three bound in one volume with a decorative cloth cover, end papers, and a newly written and designed preface and title-page. 3s. 6d. net; separately 9d. net each.

Custance (Olive).
  FIRST FRUITS: Poems. Fcap. 8vo. 3s. 6d. net.

Dalmon (C. W.).
  SONG FAVOURS. With a Title-page by J. P. DONNE. Sq. 16mo. 3s. 6d. net.

Davidson (John).
  PLAYS: An Unhistorical Pastoral; A Romantic Farce; Bruce, a Chronicle Play; Smith, a Tragic Farce; Scaramouch in Naxos, a Pantomime. With a Frontispiece and Cover Design by AUBREY BEARDSLEY. Small 4to. 7s. 6d. net.
  FLEET STREET ECLOGUES. Fcap. 8vo, buckram. 4s. 6d. net. [*Third Edition.*
  FLEET STREET ECLOGUES. 2nd Series. Fcap. 8vo, buckram. 4s. 6d. net. [*Second Edition.*
  A RANDOM ITINERARY AND A BALLAD. With a Frontispiece and Title-page by LAURENCE HOUSMAN. Fcap. 8vo, Irish Linen. 5s. net.
  BALLADS AND SONGS. With a Title-page and Cover Design by WALTER WEST. Fcap. 8vo, buckram. 5s. net. [*Fourth Edition.*
  NEW BALLADS. Fcap. 8vo, buckram. 4s. 6d. net.

De Tabley (Lord)
  POEMS, DRAMATIC AND LYRICAL. By JOHN LEICESTER WARREN (Lord de Tabley). Illustrations and Cover Design by C. S. RICKETTS. Crown 8vo. 7s. 6d. net. [*Third Edition.*
  POEMS, DRAMATIC AND LYRICAL. Second Series, uniform in binding with the former volume. Crown 8vo. 5s. net.

Duer (Caroline, and Alice).
  POEMS. Fcap. 8vo. 3s. 6d. net.

Egerton (George)
  KEYNOTES. (*See* KEYNOTES SERIES.)
  DISCORDS. (*See* KEYNOTES SERIES.)
  YOUNG OFEG'S DITTIES. A translation from the Swedish of OLA HANSSON. With Title-page and Cover Design by AUBREY BEARDSLEY. Crown 8vo. 3s. 6d. net.
  SYMPHONIES. [*In preparation.*

Eglinton (John).
TWO ESSAYS ON THE REMNANT. Post 8vo, wrappers. 1s. 6d. net. *Transferred to the present Publisher.* [*Second Edition.*]

Eve's Library.
Each volume, crown 8vo. 3s. 6d. net.
  I. MODERN WOMEN. An English rendering of LAURA MARHOLM HANSSON'S "DAS BUCH DER FRAUEN" by HERMIONE RAMSDEN. Subjects: Sonia Kovalevsky, George Egerton, Eleanora Duse, Amalie Skram, Marie Bashkirtseff, A. Ch. Edgren Leffler.
  II. THE ASCENT OF WOMAN. By ROY DEVEREUX.
  III. MARRIAGE QUESTIONS IN MODERN FICTION. By ELIZABETH RACHEL CHAPMAN.

Fea (Allan).
THE FLIGHT OF THE KING: a full, true, and particular account of the escape of His Most Sacred Majesty King Charles II. after the Battle of Worcester, with Twelve Portraits in Photogravure and nearly 100 other Illustrations. Demy 8vo. 21s. net.

Field (Eugene).
THE LOVE AFFAIRS OF A BIBLIOMANIAC. Post 8vo. 3s. 6d. net.

Fletcher (J. S.).
THE WONDERFUL WAPENTAKE. By "A SON OF THE SOIL." With 18 full-page Illustrations by J. A. SYMINGTON. Crown 8vo. 5s. 6d. net.
LIFE IN ARCADIA. (*See* ARCADY LIBRARY.)
GOD'S FAILURES. (*See* KEYNOTES SERIES.)
BALLADS OF REVOLT. Sq. 32mo. 2s. 6d. net.

Ford (James L.).
THE LITERARY SHOP AND OTHER TALES. Fcap. 8vo. 3s. 6d. net.

Four-and-Sixpenny Novels
Each volume with Title-page and Cover Design by PATTEN WILSON. Crown 8vo. 4s. 6d. net.
GALLOPING DICK. By H. B. MARRIOTT WATSON.
THE WOOD OF THE BRAMBLES. By FRANK MATHEW.
THE SACRIFICE OF FOOLS. By R. MANIFOLD CRAIG.
A LAWYER'S WIFE. By Sir NEVILL GEARY, Bart. [*Second Edition.*]
The following are in preparation :
WEIGHED IN THE BALANCE. By HARRY LANDER.
GLAMOUR. By META ORRED.
PATIENCE SPARHAWK AND HER TIMES. By GERTRUDE ATHERTON.
THE WISE AND THE WAYWARD. By G. S. STREET.
MIDDLE GREYNESS. By A. J. DAWSON.
THE MARTYR'S BIBLE. By GEORGE FIFTH.
A CELIBATE'S WIFE. By HERBERT FLOWERDEW.
MAX. By JULIAN CROSKEY.

Fuller (H. B.).
THE PUPPET BOOTH. Twelve Plays. Crown 8vo. 4s. 6d. net.

Gale (Norman).
ORCHARD SONGS. With Title-page and Cover Design by J. ILLINGWORTH KAY. Fcap. 8vo, Irish Linen. 5s. net.
Also a Special Edition limited in number on hand-made paper bound in English vellum. £1 1s. net.

Garnett (Richard).
POEMS. With Title-page by J. ILLINGWORTH KAY. Crown 8vo. 5s. net.
DANTE, PETRARCH, CAMOENS, cxxiv Sonnets, rendered in English. With Title-page by PATTEN WILSON. Crown 8vo. 5s. net.

Gibson (Charles Dana).
PICTURES : Eighty-Five Large Cartoons. Oblong Folio. 15s. net.
PICTURES OF PEOPLE. Eighty-Five Large Cartoons. Oblong folio. 15s. net.
[*In preparation.*

Gosse (Edmund).
THE LETTERS OF THOMAS LOVELL BEDDOES. Now first edited. Pott 8vo. 5s. net.
Also 25 copies large paper. 17s. 6d. net.

Grahame (Kenneth).
PAGAN PAPERS. With Title-page by AUBREY BEARDSLEY. Fcap. 8vo. 5s. net.
[Out of Print at present.
THE GOLDEN AGE. With Cover Design by CHARLES ROBINSON. Crown 8vo. 3s. 6d. net.
[Fifth Edition.

Greene (G. A.).
ITALIAN LYRISTS OF TO-DAY. Translations in the original metres from about thirty-five living Italian poets, with bibliographical and biographical notes. Crown 8vo. 5s. net.

Greenwood (Frederick).
IMAGINATION IN DREAMS. Crown 8vo. 5s. net.

Hake (T. Gordon).
A SELECTION FROM HIS POEMS. Edited by Mrs. MEYNELL. With a Portrait after D. G. ROSSETTI, and a Cover Design by GLEESON WHITE. Crown 8vo. 5s. net.

Hayes (Alfred).
THE VALE OF ARDEN AND OTHER POEMS. With a Title-page and a Cover designed by E. H. NEW. Fcap. 8vo. 3s. 6d. net.
Also 25 copies large paper. 15s. net.

Hazlitt (William).
LIBER AMORIS; OR, THE NEW PYGMALION. Edited, with an Introduction, by RICHARD LE GALLIENNE. To which is added an exact transcript of the original MS., Mrs. Hazlitt's Diary in Scotland, and letters never before published. Portrait after BEWICK, and facsimile letters. 400 Copies only. 4to, 364 pp., buckram. 21s. net.

Heinemann (William).
THE FIRST STEP; A Dramatic Moment. Small 4to. 3s. 6d. net.

Hopper (Nora).
BALLADS IN PROSE. With a Title-page and Cover by WALTER WEST. Sq. 16mo. 5s. net.
UNDER QUICKEN BOUGHS. With Title-page designed by PATTEN WILSON, and Cover designed by ELIZABETH NAYLOR. Crown 8vo. 5s. net.

Housman (Clemence).
THE WERE WOLF. With 6 full-page Illustrations, Title-page, and Cover Design by LAURENCE HOUSMAN. Sq. 16mo. 3s. 6d. net.

Housman (Laurence).
GREEN ARRAS: Poems. With 6 Illustrations, Title-page, Cover Design, and End Papers by the Author. Crown 8vo. 5s. net.
GODS AND THEIR MAKERS. Crown 8vo, 5s. net. *[In preparation.*

Irving (Laurence).
GODEFROI AND YOLANDE: A Play. Sm. 4to. 3s. 6d. net.
[In preparation.

James (W. P.)
ROMANTIC PROFESSIONS: A Volume of Essays. With Title-page designed by J. ILLINGWORTH KAY. Crown 8vo. 5s. net.

Johnson (Lionel).
THE ART OF THOMAS HARDY: Six Essays. With Etched Portrait by WM. STRANG, and Bibliography by JOHN LANE. Crown 8vo. 5s. 6d. net. *[Second Edition.*
Also 150 copies, large paper, with proofs of the portrait. £1 1s. net.

Johnson (Pauline).
WHITE WAMPUM: Poems. With a Title-page and Cover Design by E. H. NEW. Crown 8vo. 5s. net.

Johnstone (C. E.).
BALLADS OF BOY AND BEAK. With a Title-page by F. H. TOWNSEND. Sq. 32mo. 2s. net.

Keynotes Series.

Each volume with specially-designed Title-page by AUBREY BEARDSLEY or PATTEN WILSON. Crown 8vo, cloth. 3s. 6d. net.

I. KEYNOTES. By GEORGE EGERTON.
   [Seventh Edition.
II. THE DANCING FAUN. By FLORENCE FARR.
III. POOR FOLK. Translated from the Russian of F. Dostoievsky by LENA MILMAN. With a Preface by GEORGE MOORE.
IV. A CHILD OF THE AGE. By FRANCIS ADAMS.
V. THE GREAT GOD PAN AND THE INMOST LIGHT. By ARTHUR MACHEN.
   [Second Edition.
VI. DISCORDS. By GEORGE EGERTON.
   [Fifth Edition.
VII. PRINCE ZALESKI. By M. P. SHIEL.
VIII. THE WOMAN WHO DID. By GRANT ALLEN.
   [Twenty-second Edition.
IX. WOMEN'S TRAGEDIES. By H. D. LOWRY.
X. GREY ROSES. By HENRY HARLAND.
XI. AT THE FIRST CORNER AND OTHER STORIES. By H. B. MARRIOTT WATSON.
XII. MONOCHROMES. By ELLA D'ARCY.
XIII. AT THE RELTON ARMS. By EVELYN SHARP.
XIV. THE GIRL FROM THE FARM. By GERTRUDE DIX.
   [Second Edition.
XV. THE MIRROR OF MUSIC. By STANLEY V. MAKOWER.
XVI. YELLOW AND WHITE. By W. CARLTON DAWE.
XVII. THE MOUNTAIN LOVERS. By FIONA MACLEOD.
XVIII. THE WOMAN WHO DIDN'T. By VICTORIA CROSSE.
   [Third Edition.

Keynotes Series—*continued.*

XIX. THE THREE IMPOSTORS. By ARTHUR MACHEN.
XX. NOBODY'S FAULT. By NETTA SYRETT.
   [Second Edition.
XXI. THE BRITISH BARBARIANS. By GRANT ALLEN.
   [Second Edition.
XXII. IN HOMESPUN. By E. NESBIT.
XXIII. PLATONIC AFFECTIONS. By JOHN SMITH.
XXIV. NETS FOR THE WIND. By UNA TAYLOR.
XXV. WHERE THE ATLANTIC MEETS THE LAND. By CALDWELL LIPSETT.
XXVI. IN SCARLET AND GREY. By FLORENCE HENNIKER. (With THE SPECTRE OF THE REAL by FLORENCE HENNIKER and THOMAS HARDY.) *[Second Edition.*
XXVII. MARIS STELLA. By MARIE CLOTHILDE BALFOUR.
XXVIII. DAY BOOKS. By MABEL E. WOTTON.
XXIX. SHAPES IN THE FIRE. By M. P. SHIEL.
XXX. UGLY IDOL. By CLAUD NICHOLSON.

The following are in rapid preparation:

XXXI. KAKEMONOS. By W. CARLTON DAWE.
XXXII. GOD'S FAILURES. By J. S. FLETCHER.
XXXIII. A DELIVERANCE. By ALLAN MONKHOUSE.
XXXIV. MERE SENTIMENT. By A. J. DAWSON.

Lane's Library.

Each volume crown 8vo. 3s. 6d. net.

I. MARCH HARES. By GEORGE FORTH.
   [Second Edition.
II. THE SENTIMENTAL SEX. By GERTRUDE WARDEN.
III. GOLD. By ANNIE LINDEN.

THE PUBLICATIONS OF

Lane's Library—*continued.*

The following are in preparation:
- IV. BROKEN AWAY. By BEATRICE GRIMSHAW.
- V. RICHARD LARCH. By E. A. BENNETT.
- VI. THE DUKE OF LINDEN. By JOSEPH F. CHARLES.

Leather (R. K.).
VERSES. 250 copies. Fcap. 8vo. 3s. net. [*Transferred to the present Publisher.*

Lefroy (Edward Cracroft.)
POEMS. With a Memoir by W. A. GILL, and a reprint of Mr. J. A. SYMONDS' Critical Essay on "Echoes from Theocritus." Cr. 8vo. Photogravure Portrait. 5s. net.

Le Gallienne (Richard).
PROSE FANCIES. With Portrait of the Author by WILSON STEER. Crown 8vo. Purple cloth. 5s. net. [*Fourth Edition.*
Also a limited large paper edition. 12s. 6d. net.

THE BOOK BILLS OF NARCISSUS. An Account rendered by RICHARD LE GALLIENNE. With a Frontispiece. Crown 8vo, purple cloth. 3s. 6d. net. [*Third Edition.*
Also 50 copies on large paper. 8vo. 10s. 6d. net.

ROBERT LOUIS STEVENSON, AN ELEGY, AND OTHER POEMS, MAINLY PERSONAL. With Etched Title-page by D. Y. CAMERON. Crown 8vo, purple cloth. 4s. 6d. net.
Also 75 copies on large paper. 8vo. 12s. 6d. net.

ENGLISH POEMS. Crown 8vo, purple cloth. 4s. 6d. net.
[*Fourth Edition, revised.*

GEORGE MEREDITH : Some Characteristics. With a Bibliography (much enlarged) by JOHN LANE, portrait, &c. Crown 8vo, purple cloth. 5s. 6d. net.
[*Fourth Edition.*

Le Gallienne (Richard)—*continued.*
THE RELIGION OF A LITERARY MAN. Crown 8vo, purple cloth. 3s. 6d. net. [*Fifth Thousand.*
Also a special rubricated edition on hand-made paper. 8vo. 10s. 6d. net.

RETROSPECTIVE REVIEWS, A LITERARY LOG, 1891-1895. 2 vols. Crown 8vo, purple cloth. 9s. net.

PROSE FANCIES. (Second Series). Crown 8vo, Purple cloth. 5s. net.

THE QUEST OF THE GOLDEN GIRL. Crown 8vo. 5s. net.
[*In preparation.*
See also HAZLITT, WALTON and COTTON.

Lowry (H. D.).
MAKE BELIEVE. Illustrated by CHARLES ROBINSON. Crown 8vo, gilt edges or uncut. 5s. net.
WOMEN'S TRAGEDIES. (*See* KEYNOTES SERIES).

Lucas (Winifred).
UNITS : Poems. Fcap. 8vo. 3s. 6d. net.

Lynch (Hannah).
THE GREAT GALEOTO AND FOLLY OR SAINTLINESS. Two Plays, from the Spanish of JOSÉ ECHEGARAY, with an Introduction. Small 4to. 5s. 6d. net.

Marzials (Theo.).
THE GALLERY OF PIGEONS AND OTHER POEMS. Post 8vo. 4s. 6d. net. [*Transferred to the present Publisher.*

The Mayfair Set.
Each volume fcap. 8vo. 3s. 6d. net.
I. THE AUTOBIOGRAPHY OF A BOY. Passages selected by his friend G. S. STREET. With a Title-page designed by C. W. FURSE.
[*Fifth Edition.*
II. THE JONESES AND THE ASTERISKS. A Story in Monologue. By GERALD CAMPBELL. With a Title-page and 6 Illustrations by F. H. TOWNSEND.
[*Second Edition.*

The Mayfair Set—*continued*.
  III. SELECT CONVERSATIONS WITH AN UNCLE. NOW EXTINCT. By H. G. WELLS. With a Title-page by F. H. TOWNSEND.
  IV. FOR PLAIN WOMEN ONLY. By GEORGE FLEMING. With a Title-page by PATTEN WILSON.
  V. THE FEASTS OF AUTOLYCUS: THE DIARY OF A GREEDY WOMAN. Edited by ELIZABETH ROBINS PENNELL. With a Title-page by PATTEN WILSON.
  VI. MRS. ALBERT GRUNDY: OBSERVATIONS IN PHILISTIA. By HAROLD FREDERIC. With a Title-page by PATTEN WILSON. [*Second Edition.*

Meredith (George).
THE FIRST PUBLISHED PORTRAIT OF THIS AUTHOR, engraved on the wood by W. BISCOMBE GARDNER, after the painting by G. F. WATTS. Proof copies on Japanese vellum, signed by painter and engraver. £1 1s. net.

Meynell (Mrs.).
POEMS. Fcap. 8vo. 3s. 6d. net. [*Fourth Edition.*
THE RHYTHM OF LIFE AND OTHER ESSAYS. Fcap. 8vo. 3s. 6d. net. [*Third Edition.*
THE COLOUR OF LIFE AND OTHER ESSAYS. Fcap. 8vo. 3s. 6d. net. [*Second Edition.*
THE DARLING YOUNG. Fcap. 8vo. 3s. 6d. net. [*In preparation.*

Miller (Joaquin).
THE BUILDING OF THE CITY BEAUTIFUL. Fcap. 8vo. With a Decorated Cover. 5s. net.

Money-Coutts (F. B.).
POEMS. With Title-page designed by PATTEN WILSON. Crown 8vo. 3s. 6d. net.

Monkhouse (Allan).
BOOKS AND PLAYS: A Volume of Essays on Meredith, Borrow, Ibsen, and others. Crown 8vo. 5s. net.

Nesbit (E.).
A POMANDER OF VERSE. With a Title-page and Cover designed by LAURENCE HOUSMAN. Crown 8vo. 5s. net.
IN HOMESPUN. (*See* KEYNOTES SERIES.)

Nettleship (J. T.).
ROBERT BROWNING: Essays and Thoughts. Crown 8vo. 5s. 6d. net. [*Third Edition.*

Noble (Jas. Ashcroft).
THE SONNET IN ENGLAND AND OTHER ESSAYS. Title-page and Cover Design by AUSTIN YOUNG. Crown 8vo. 5s. net.
Also 50 copies large paper 12s. 6d. net

Oppenheim (Michael).
A HISTORY OF THE ADMINISTRATION OF THE ROYAL NAVY, and of Merchant Shipping in relation to the Navy from MDIX to MDCLX, with an introduction treating of the earlier period. With Illustrations. Demy 8vo. 15s. net.

O'Shaughnessy (Arthur).
HIS LIFE AND HIS WORK. With Selections from his Poems. By LOUISE CHANDLER MOULTON. Portrait and Cover Design. Fcap. 8vo. 5s. net.

Oxford Characters.
A series of lithographed portraits by WILL ROTHENSTEIN, with text by F. YORK POWELL and others. 200 copies only, folio, buckram. £3 3s. net.
25 special large paper copies containing proof impressions of the portraits signed by the artist, £6 6s. net.

Peters (Wm. Theodore).
POSIES OUT OF RINGS. With Title-page by PATTEN WILSON. Sq. 16mo. 2s. 6d. net.

Pierrot's Library.
Each volume with Title-page, Cover and End Papers, designed by AUBREY BEARDSLEY. Sq. 16mo. 2s. net.
  I. PIERROT. By H. DE VERE STACPOOLE.
  II. MY LITTLE LADY ANNE. By MRS. EGERTON CASTLE.
  III. SIMPLICITY. By A. T. G. PRICE.
  IV. MY BROTHER. By VINCENT BROWN.

The following are in preparation:
  V. DEATH, THE KNIGHT, AND THE LADY. By H. DE VERE STACPOOLE.
  VI. MR. PASSINGHAM. By THOMAS COBB.
  VII. TWO IN CAPTIVITY. By VINCENT BROWN.

Plarr (Victor).
IN THE DORIAN MOOD: Poems. With Title-page by PATTEN WILSON. Crown 8vo. 5s. net.

Radford (Dollie).
SONGS AND OTHER VERSES. With a Title-page by PATTEN WILSON. Fcap. 8vo. 4s. 6d. net.

Rhys (Ernest).
A LONDON ROSE AND OTHER RHYMES. With Title-page designed by SELWYN IMAGE. Crown 8vo. 5s. net.

Robertson (John M.).
ESSAYS TOWARDS A CRITICAL METHOD. (New Series.) Crown 8vo. 5s. net. [*In preparation.*

St. Cyres (Lord).
THE LITTLE FLOWERS OF ST. FRANCIS: A new rendering into English of the Fioretti di San Francesco. Crown 8vo. 5s. net. [*In preparation.*

Seaman (Owen).
THE BATTLE OF THE BAYS. Fcap. 8vo. 3s. 6d. net.

Sedgwick (Jane Minot).
SONGS FROM THE GREEK. Fcap. 8vo. 3s. 6d. net.

Setoun (Gabriel).
THE CHILD WORLD: Poems. Illustrated by CHARLES ROBINSON. Crown 8vo. gilt edges or uncut. 5s. net. [*In preparation.*

Sharp (Evelyn).
WYMPS: Fairy Tales. With Coloured Illustrations by MABEL DEARMER. Small 4to, decorated cover. 4s. 6d. net. [*In preparation.*
AT THE RELTON ARMS. (*See* KEYNOTES SERIES.)

Shore (Louisa).
POEMS. With an appreciation by FREDERIC HARRISON and a Portrait. Fcap. 8vo. 5s. net.

Short Stories Series.
Each volume Post 8vo. Coloured edges. 2s. 6d. net.
  I. THE HINT O' HAIRST. By MÉNIE MURIEL DOWIE.
  II. THE SENTIMENTAL VIKINGS. By R. V. RISLEY.
  III. SHADOWS OF LIFE. By Mrs. MURRAY HICKSON.

Stevenson (Robert Louis).
PRINCE OTTO. A Rendering in French by EGERTON CASTLE. With Frontispiece, Title-page, and Cover Design by D. Y. CAMERON. Crown 8vo. 7s. 6d. net.
Also 50 copies on large paper, uniform in size with the Edinburgh Edition of the Works.
A CHILD'S GARDEN OF VERSES. With over 150 Illustrations by CHARLES ROBINSON. Crown 8vo. 5s. net. [*Second Edition.*

Stoddart (Thos. Tod).
THE DEATH WAKE. With an Introduction by ANDREW LANG. Fcap. 8vo. 5s. net.

Street (G. S.).
EPISODES. Post 8vo. 3s. net.
MINIATURES AND MOODS. Fcap. 8vo. 3s. net. [*Both transferred to the present Publisher.*
QUALES EGO: A FEW REMARKS, IN PARTICULAR AND AT LARGE. Fcap. 8vo. 3s. 6d. net.

Street (G. S.)—*continued.*
  THE AUTOBIOGRAPHY OF A BOY.
  (*See* MAYFAIR SET.)
  THE WISE AND THE WAYWARD.
  (*See* FOUR - AND - SIXPENNY NOVELS.)

Swettenham (F. A.)
  MALAY SKETCHES. With a Title-page and Cover Design by PATTEN WILSON. Crown 8vo. 5s. net.
  [*Second Edition.*

Tabb (John B.).
  POEMS. Sq. 32mo. 4s. 6d. net.

Tennyson (Frederick).
  POEMS OF THE DAY AND YEAR. With a Title-page designed by PATTEN WILSON. Crown 8vo. 5s. net.

Thimm (Carl A.).
  A COMPLETE BIBLIOGRAPHY OF FENCING AND DUELLING, AS PRACTISED BY ALL EUROPEAN NATIONS FROM THE MIDDLE AGES TO THE PRESENT DAY. With a Classified Index, arranged Chronologically according to Languages. Illustrated with numerous Portraits of Ancient and Modern Masters of the Art. Title-pages and Frontispieces of some of the earliest works. Portrait of the Author by WILSON STEER, and Title-page designed by PATTEN WILSON. 4to. 21s. net.

Thompson (Francis).
  POEMS. With Frontispiece, Title-page, and Cover Design by LAURENCE HOUSMAN. Pott 4to. 5s. net. [*Fourth Edition.*
  SISTER-SONGS: An Offering to Two Sisters. With Frontispiece, Title-page, and Cover Design by LAURENCE HOUSMAN. Pott 4to. 5s. net.

Thoreau (Henry David).
  POEMS OF NATURE. Selected and edited by HENRY S. SALT and FRANK B. SANBORN, with a Title-page designed by PATTEN WILSON. Fcap. 8vo. 4s. 6d. net.

Traill (H. D.).
  THE BARBAROUS BRITISHERS: A Tip-top Novel. With Title and Cover Design by AUBREY BEARDSLEY. Crown 8vo, wrapper. 1s. net.
  FROM CAIRO TO THE SOUDAN FRONTIER. With Cover Design by PATTEN WILSON. Crown 8vo. 5s. net.

Tynan Hinkson (Katharine).
  CUCKOO SONGS. With Title-page and Cover Design by LAURENCE HOUSMAN. Fcap. 8vo. 5s. net.
  MIRACLE PLAYS. OUR LORD'S COMING AND CHILDHOOD. With 6 Illustrations, Title-page, and Cover Design by PATTEN WILSON. Fcap. 8vo. 4s. 6d. net.

Walton and Cotton.
  THE COMPLEAT ANGLER. Edited by RICHARD LE GALLIENNE. Illustrated by EDMUND H. NEW. Crown 4to, decorated cover. 15s. net.
  Also to be had in twelve 1s. parts.

Watson (Rosamund Marriott).
  VESPERTILIA AND OTHER POEMS. With a Title-page designed by R. ANNING BELL. Fcap. 8vo. 4s. 6d. net.
  A SUMMER NIGHT AND OTHER POEMS. New Edition. With a Decorative Title-page. Fcap. 8vo. 3s. net.

Watson (William).
  THE FATHER OF THE FOREST AND OTHER POEMS. With New Photogravure Portrait of the Author Fcap. 8vo, buckram. 3s. 6d. net.
  [*Fifth Edition.*
  ODES AND OTHER POEMS. Fcap. 8vo, buckram. 4s. 6d. net.
  [*Fourth Edition.*
  THE ELOPING ANGELS: A Caprice Square 16mo, buckram. 3s. 6d. net. [*Second Edition.*
  EXCURSIONS IN CRITICISM: being some Prose Recreations of a Rhymer. Crown 8vo, buckram. 5s. net. • [*Second Edition.*

Watson (William)—*continued.*
THE PRINCE'S QUEST AND OTHER POEMS. With a Bibliographical Note added. Fcap. 8vo, buckram. 4s. 6d. net. [*Third Edition.*
THE PURPLE EAST: A Series of Sonnets on England's Desertion of Armenia. With a Frontispiece after G. F. WATTS, R.A. Fcap. 8vo, wrappers. 1s. net.
[*Third Edition.*

Watt (Francis).
THE LAW'S LUMBER ROOM. Fcap. 8vo. 3s. 6d. net.
[*Second Edition.*

Watts-Dunton (Theodore).
POEMS. Crown 8vo. 5s. net.
[*In preparation.*
There will also be an *Edition de Luxe* of this volume printed at the Kelmscott Press.

Wharton (H. T.)
SAPPHO. Memoir, Text, Selected Renderings, and a Literal Translation by HENRY THORNTON WHARTON. With 3 Illustrations in Photogravure, and a Cover designed by AUBREY BEARDSLEY. Fcap. 8vo. 7s. 6d. net. [*Third Edition.*

THE YELLOW BOOK

An Illustrated Quarterly.

Pott 4to. 5s. net.

I. April 1894, 272 pp., 15 Illustrations. [*Out of print.*
II. July 1894, 364 pp., 23 Illustrations.
III. October 1894, 280 pp., 15 Illustrations.
IV. January 1895, 285 pp., 16 Illustrations.
V. April 1895, 317 pp., 14 Illustrations.
VI. July 1895, 335 pp., 16 Illustrations.
VII. October 1895, 320 pp., 20 Illustrations.
VIII. January 1896, 406 pp., 26 Illustrations.
IX. April 1896, 256 pp., 17 Illustrations.
X. July 1896, 340 pp., 13 Illustrations.

www.ingramcontent.com/pod-product-compliance
Lightning Source LLC
Chambersburg PA
CBHW020155170426
43199CB00010B/1044